JUNIOR SURVIVAL LIBRARY
Hunter in the sky

THE EAGLE

Malcolm Penny

ANGLIA
Television Limited

Boxtree

Key to abbreviations

lb	pound
kg	kilogram
in	inch
ft	foot
yd	yard
cm	centimetre
m	metre
km	kilometre
sq mile	square mile
sq km	square kilometre
kph	kilometres per hour
mph	miles per hour

First published in 1990 by Boxtree Limited
Copyright © 1990 Survival Anglia Limited
Text copyright © 1990 Malcolm Penny

Front jacket photographs: Survival Anglia/Jeff Foot
(Bald eagle with fish)
Survival Anglia/Dieter & Mary Plage
(White-bellied sea eagle swooping down on a fish)
Back jacket photograph: Survival Anglia/Richard & Julia Kemp
(Short-toed eagle eating a snake)

Line drawings by Raymond Turvey

British Library Cataloguing in Publication Data
Penny, Malcolm
  The eagle.
  I. Title II. Series
  598.916

ISBN 1-85283-055-7

Edited by Miranda Smith
Designed by Groom & Pickerill
Typeset by Rowland Phototypesetting Limited
Bury St Edmunds, Suffolk

Printed and bound in Italy
by OFSA S.p.A.

for Boxtree Limited,
36 Tavistock Street,
London WC2E 7PB

Contents

What is an eagle? 4

How eagles feed 6

Fishing eagles 8

Snake eagles 10

Forest eagles 12

Large but not safe 14

Courtship and nesting 16

The new generation 18

Space for eagles 20

Travelling eagles 22

Beliefs and fables 24

Threats to eagles 26

Protecting eagles 28

Glossary and Notes on Author 30

Index 31

Acknowledgements 32

What is an eagle?

Eagles are birds of prey, which means that they live by hunting other animals. Birds of prey live all over the world, in many different **habitats**. They have certain things in common because of the way in which they get their food. They hunt by day. They have very good eyesight, to spot their prey, often from high in the air. They can all fly very fast, to attack before they are seen. They have powerful **talons**, with which to grasp their **prey**. They also have sharp, hooked beaks with which to tear up their prey when they have caught it.

Some examples of birds of prey are hawks, buzzards, falcons and vultures. Owls are not strictly birds of prey because they fly at night. However, they do catch animals to eat.

The biggest of all the birds of prey are the eagles. Eagles live in all the parts of the world where there are animals for them to catch. Some of them feed on other birds, some on small **mammals**, and some on unexpected food such as fish or snakes.

Most eagles need plenty of space so that they can find enough food, especially when they are rearing their chicks. This can cause

An eagle's talons are strong and very sharp, they are used for gripping hold of prey.

Tools of the eagle's trade

An eagle's beak needs to be strong as well as sharp to catch its prey. This is why the upper jaw is so deep, it means that the bird can bite hard without its beak bending.

The talons are curved so that they meet in the middle of the prey's body. It is practically impossible for a victim to escape once the eagle has a good grip.

The eyes of an eagle are not set at the sides of its head, like those of most other birds, but in front, so that it can look at its prey with both eyes at once. This is called 'binocular vision', and it enables the bird to judge distance, and so to hit the prey more accurately.

The eyes and beak of a young eagle are just as powerful as those of an adult.

problems for them, because land which is used for farming or is covered in buildings may not have enough prey animals on it. Eagles are also in danger because some people are afraid of them, or blame them for stealing lambs, and so try to kill them.

In this book, we shall meet many different kinds of eagles, to find out where and how they live. We shall also see what problems they have, and what can be done to protect their habitats and make them safe.

How eagles feed

Eagles glide with outspread wings, watching the ground very carefully as they look for an animal to eat. They hunt entirely by sight, and not by smell or sound like many other **predators**.

All birds of prey have very good eyesight. Because of the arrangement of the cells in the **retina** of their eyes, they can see at least four times as well as humans. An African buzzard was once seen catching a grasshopper which it had spotted from over 100 m (320 ft) away.

Eagles catch their prey by means of a sudden dive, called a 'stoop'. To dive upon a victim as fast as possible, an eagle folds its wings closer to its body when it stoops.

When it gets close to the prey, the eagle reaches out its legs, and grips the victim in its strong claws. The back talon digs into the victim's body, and the others close up, to take a firm grip. The eagle then spreads its wide, strong wings to lift the prey off the ground.

A white-bellied sea eagle glides high over an African lake searching for fish.

Above *A verreaux' eagle flies with a captured rock hyrax in its talons.*

Right *A tawny eagle mantles its prey with its wings before starting to feed.*

Most eagles carry their prey a little way before feeding on it. Many of them cover the victim with their wings when they start to feed. This is called 'mantling', but nobody really knows yet why they do it.

An eagle's beak is very sharp, and hooked at the end, so that it can tear up its food. The sides of the beak are often curved, rather like the blades of a pair of kitchen scissors. This makes it easier for the eagle to cut the skin and **tendons** of its victim.

Most eagles catch small or middle-sized mammals, such as rabbits or **hyraxes**, but some of them specialise in different kinds of food.

Fishing eagles

One of the most spectacular sights in Africa is to see a fish eagle snatching its prey from a lake. It cannot catch fish which are deep in the water, so it glides quite high up, watching for the glint of scales near the surface.

When it spots a fish that is within reach, the fish eagle dives down, flattening out at the last moment and pushing its feet forward, with its talons outstretched. It very rarely misses its target.

One of the favourite foods of a fish eagle is the catfish, which can breathe air as well as using its **gills** to breathe under the water. Catfish often come to the surface to breathe. If an eagle sees the ripples they make, it will attack.

Sometimes, the fish an eagle has caught is too big for the bird to lift out of the water. This can be very awkward for the eagle, because its claws are made in such a way that it is difficult for it to let go once it has caught a fish.

The white-bellied sea eagle is a skilful hunter, rarely missing its chosen target.

Sometimes a fish eagle is pulled under the water by a particularly big fish, until it can work its talons loose.

Fish eagles eat other food as well as fish. They catch water birds, especially young cormorants, herons and spoonbills, which they take from their nesting **colonies**.

In North America, there is a large eagle which looks like the African fish eagle, but is not such a good hunter. It is called the bald eagle, and it is the national bird of America. It is called 'bald' because it is black and white, like a piebald horse. Bald eagles are mainly **scavengers**, flying down to feed on dead fish and other **carrion** by the water's edge.

Feeding fish eagles

On Lake Malawi, when the fishing boats return from a day's work, several of the local fish eagles follow them into harbour, just as gulls follow fishing boats into sea ports. This is because some of the fishermen throw fish up into the air, to watch the eagles catch them. Like most hunting animals, eagles are very quick to learn, and take advantage of anything which makes their lives easier.

The American bald eagle is more of a scavenger than a hunter.

Snake eagles

In Africa and India, there are several species of eagle which specialise in feeding on snakes. They are different from other eagles in several ways. They have rather long legs, with thick, smooth scales. They also have short toes, and the soles of their feet are rough. All these features help them to catch and hold their often dangerous prey.

Snake eagles also have extraordinary eyesight. Their prey is often **camouflaged**, and yet they can see it from a long way away. One snake eagle was seen to dive on a snake which it had spotted from a distance of 500 m (1,600 ft).

Snake eagles usually live in wooded or bushy areas, often along the edge of rivers that flow through dry country. They spend the day sitting high up on a dead tree, watching for prey. Sometimes they fly slowly, hovering with their heads pointing into the wind. The African short-toed eagle is the largest bird of prey which can hover in this way. By keeping its head still, it has the best chance of finding a snake on the ground below.

A brown snake eagle in Zambia watching for prey from the branch of a tree.

In Spain, a short-toed eagle grabs a grass snake which it has spotted from the air.

Snake eagles need a large **territory** in which to find their food. A pair may need as much as 200 sq kms (77 sq miles).

Although snake eagles take non-poisonous snakes if they can find them, they often catch venomous species, such as cobras and puff adders. They avoid being bitten by attacking very fast, and they are protected by the thick scales on their legs. Also, the down on their thighs and belly is very thick, so that if a snake bites a snake eagle, it is likely to get no more than a mouthful of feathers. Snake eagles are not **immune** to snake venom, and sometimes they are killed by the snakes they have attacked.

Forest eagles

The Philippine eagle is very large and powerful.

Opposite *The harpy eagle is rare in most Mexican forests.*

In dense forests, where it is dark and difficult to spot prey, the most common hunting birds are owls. Most eagles prefer to feed in open spaces, where they can move freely, and make the best use of their speed and strength. However, there are some that live in tall ancient forests, where the **canopy** is high enough above the ground for them to fly easily beneath it. One example is the Philippine eagle, once known as the monkey-eating eagle.

It is an enormous bird, with a **wingspan** of nearly 2m (6ft), but it is very agile and fast as it flies through the forest. In spite of its name, it preys on other mammals as well as monkeys. Sloths, slow-moving animals the size of collie dogs, which climb in the trees, are often caught and killed by Philippine eagles.

Sadly, the Philippine eagle is now very rare. There may be less than 100 left in the Philippine Islands. Their forest home has been disturbed or destroyed by people, and they are hunted as a **trophy**.

Harpy eagles live on the mainland of South America, in the same type of ancient forest as the Philippine eagle. Although they are hunted in the same way, they are still fairly common. However, the forests where they live are being cut down for timber and to make farmland.

In Africa, the crowned eagle and the Congo serpent eagle live successfully even in the thickest forests. The eagles hunt by day, and the owls by night, so that the small animals of the forest floor are in constant danger.

Large but not safe

When people think of eagles, it is usually the largest and strongest which come to mind, huge birds with broad wings, gliding effortlessly over open mountainsides, stooping on their prey from enormous heights. In Britain, the golden eagle is the largest bird of prey, often seen soaring over the wild, dramatic scenery of the Scottish Highlands.

Golden eagles were once much more common. They lived all over the **northern hemisphere**, until humans almost wiped them out in eastern parts of North America and most of Europe. They were killed because people thought that they preyed on lambs and other domestic animals.

People feared and respected the strength of the golden eagle.

Now the golden eagle is found only in places where few people live, in Scotland and Scandinavia, and mountainous parts of the rest of Europe and North America.

Other large eagles live in different parts of the world. The martial eagle and the crowned eagle in Africa, the wedge-tailed eagle in Australia, and the harpy eagle in South America are all large and spectacular. They all have the same problems as the golden eagle. They need huge areas of land for their hunting territories, and they often come into conflict with the people who are trying to use that land to raise domestic animals.

A golden eagle soars among the Himalayas in Nepal.

Bald eagles are now very rare in most of the United States. Farmers shot them in the past, because they thought that the eagles were stealing their sheep and lambs. This was not fair, because the bald eagle is usually only a scavenger. When a farmer found a bald eagle eating the corpse of a lamb which had died from natural causes, he assumed that the eagle had killed it, and shot the eagle. Killing bald eagles is now against the law.

A crowned hawk eagle has captured a young gazelle.

The bald eagle is now very rare and is protected by law in the U.S.A.

Soaring and gliding

Eagles have very broad wings, so that they can **soar** on rising air currents, without having to flap their wings as often as most other birds. They need to be able to fly without effort, because they have to cover large distances when they are hunting.

The feathers at the tip of each wing, called 'primaries', can be spread out like fingers. When the eagle does this, each feather acts like a tiny extra wing, to give the bird extra lift.

Courtship and nesting

The courtship of eagles is spectacular to watch. A male and female fly together over their territory, diving and soaring. They often roll over until they are upside down, and sometimes grasp each other's feet. It looks as though each bird is trying to show the other how well it can fly.

An important purpose of courtship flights is to show other eagles that are passing by that the territory is occupied. They will have to go and find a place of their own.

When the courtship is over, the pair set about choosing a place to nest. The nest site is usually high up, often on a cliff or at the top of a dead tree. This gives the birds a good view of their territory, so that they can see any other eagles approaching. If the nest is high up, there is also less chance of predators reaching it. A pair may use the same site year after year, or they may alternate between two or more nest sites in the same territory.

The first thing to do is to build a nest, or repair an old one. Both members of the pair search for suitable building materials. Eagles are clumsy compared with other birds, simply piling large sticks into an untidy heap, rather than weaving them together. However, the nests seem to be quite strong, since they can last for many years. The eagles only have to add a few sticks to the nest each year when they return to breed.

The middle of the nest is usually lined with lighter materials, such as dry grass or twigs torn off nearby trees. Often these twigs have green leaves still on them, so that it looks as though the eagles are decorating their nest.

Above *A bald eagle's untidy nest high above the sea in Alaska.*

Opposite *An imperial eagle tears up food for its chick.*

Making friends again

Most eagles mate for life, but after breeding they fly off alone. For the rest of the year, they see other eagles only at a distance, and keep away from them.

When breeding time comes round again, a pair of birds will return separately to their territory, to meet their mate. Courtship is a very important time for each bird in the pair to learn once more not to be afraid of being close to another eagle.

The new generation

Some eagles lay only one egg, and other species lay two or three. When the eggs hatch, both parents take turns to feed the chicks, bringing food to the nest and giving it to the chicks in small pieces. Later, as their beaks and feet grow stronger, the chicks will learn to tear up their own food.

When there is not enough food for both of the chicks, one chick may die.

If there is more than one chick, the parents do not share out the food. The strongest chick, usually the first to hatch, takes all it wants until it is full up, before it lets the others feed. If there is not enough food, the smaller and weaker chicks starve. This seems cruel to us, but it is a way of producing more young eagles in years when there is plenty of food. It also gives the strongest chick the best chance when food is scarce.

Above *A booted eaglet, still downy, flaps its new wings.*

At first, the chicks are covered in **down**, but as they grow older they begin to grow proper feathers, including the flight feathers on their tail and wings. As they grow bigger, the young birds begin to stand on the edge of the nest, facing into the wind and flapping their half-grown wings.

At first, because the feathers are not fully grown, all this flapping has no effect. As the feathers grow longer and stronger, the birds begin to rise a little way above the nest. Finally, one by one, they leave the nest in longer and longer flights, and eventually fly away never to return.

The parents feed the young eagles, or eaglets, for some time after they have left the nest, but when the eaglets have learned to catch food for themselves, they are driven away by their parents.

This golden eaglet will soon be able to fly and leave the nest for ever.

Space for eagles

Above Bald eagles sitting in a flock by a salmon stream watching for prey.

Opposite The bateleur eagle is a brilliant aerobatic flier.

All birds, including eagles, defend a small territory round their nest, to protect their chicks from danger. Most eagles also defend a hunting area, which may be 200 sq kms (77 sq miles) in extent. However, they do not usually fight to defend these areas. They often make threatening noises and perform spectacular dives at intruders, but fighting is quite rare.

One reason for this may be their good eyesight. If an intruder can see the owner of a territory from a long way away, it will have plenty of time to move away before there is a fight. Eagles avoid fighting if they can, because they know that even the winner of a fight can be hurt.

If the intruder does not fly away, the owner may threaten it by flying rather slowly straight towards it, calling. This usually sends the intruder on its way at once.

Some eagles seem to be able to share hunting areas with other pairs of the same species. The bald eagle in America, and the fish eagle in Africa, are good examples of this. This apparently strange behaviour can be explained, if what the birds eat is taken into consideration.

Bald eagles are mainly scavengers. They often gather in large groups, for example when salmon are **spawning**. At this time, fish that have finished breeding die, leaving plenty of food for all the eagles. The birds often sit by the river in groups of 20 or 30. There is no need for them to try to drive each other away, since there is so much food. The same applies to fish eagles, when they live near a lake where fish are plentiful.

Travelling eagles

Some species of eagles **migrate** to other areas when they have finished breeding. This may be because the food has run out in their breeding area, or because the weather has become unsuitable. Some of them fly only short distances, from one African country to another. Other eagles fly thousands of kilometres from their breeding grounds in the north when winter approaches. They travel towards the sun along main routes which are known as 'flyways'.

One of the great American flyways passes over a place called Hawk Mountain, in Pennsylvania, where people go in spring and autumn to watch the eagles go by. It is possible to see thousands of eagles of many different species in one day. There are similar spectacular sights on the mountains of Afghanistan and Iran, as the Asian birds move to warmer climates in winter.

A tawny eagle in Africa can expect many winter visitors.

Counting eagles

It might seem easy to count eagles when they are passing a particular point on one of their main flyways, but it can be very difficult. Not only do they often fly very high, so that they are hard to identify or even see, but they usually circle as they travel, soaring in the **thermals** above mountains. In Africa, the favourite way of counting resident eagles is to drive along a road and make a note of every eagle seen.

Birds such as the steppe eagle and the spotted eagle migrate to Africa from Europe to spend the winter. However, their close relative, the tawny eagle, lives in Africa all the time. During the northern winter, the tawny eagles in Africa face a lot of competition from their visitors. However, since the tawny eagles are not breeding at the time, there is enough food for all the birds.

The numbers of migrants are astonishing; in one part of South Africa, there were 130 resident birds of prey, but in the winter there were over 8,000 visitors. When the migrants move northwards again for the summer, they time their arrival to match the breeding season of their food animals, such as hares and lemmings.

Below *Short-toed eagles migrate from Spain to spend the winter in Africa.*

Beliefs and fables

The eagle was the emblem of the Roman Empire, but long before that it was regarded as one of the gods in Sumeria, Babylon and ancient India. An eagle with two heads represents the joining together in 1472 of the two great empires of the time, the Roman and the Byzantine. An eagle still appears on the flags or **coats of arms** of modern countries.

In Christian churches, the Bible is supported by a **lectern** in the shape of an eagle. Some people say that this is because the eagle was the emblem of St John. Others claim that it is the main enemy of the snake, which is a symbol of evil in the Bible.

Archers used eagle feathers on their arrows, to make them fly fast and straight. Even today, some people wear an eagle's claw as a lucky ornament. They probably do not know that this is an old **superstition**, coming from the days when people believed that by killing an animal and eating or wearing part of it, a person could inherit some of the animal's power.

Although golden eagles and other large species occasionally kill lambs, they usually

Opposite *People watching eagles in Glacier National Park, U.S.A.*

Right *To most tribes of American Indians eagles are sacred.*

American Indians and eagles

The eagle is a very powerful symbol for most tribes of American Indians. It is associated with the sun, and with strength and courage. This is why Indian braves used to wear an eagle's feather in their headbands, and why only a chief could wear a full headdress of eagle's plumes.

hunt smaller animals. It is quite likely that hungry shepherds used to blame an eagle for stealing lambs, when they had eaten them themselves.

In Texas, in the United States, **ranchers** still shoot and poison eagles because they think that they steal lambs. They do this especially when large numbers of eagles are migrating through the state. One scientist worked out that even if all the migrant eagles ate nothing but freshly-killed lambs, they would only take a small part of the huge numbers available. In fact, eagles in Texas eat mostly rabbits and hares. Indeed, they are helping the ranchers, since rabbits and hares eat the grass that the sheep are supposed to eat.

Threats to eagles

It is against the law to kill eagles in most countries, although angry farmers will break the law because they see them as enemies. Deliberate killing in the past was what made eagles so rare in the eastern United States and in most of Europe. Now there are much more serious threats to eagles.

Loss of habitat may be the worst danger.

Where forests are cut down, and wilderness is turned into farmland and cities, eagles cannot find the large hunting territories that most of them need.

The next most serious threat comes from **pesticides**. Poisons used to kill insects get into the animals which eat those insects. The poisons build up in the animals, instead of passing out of their bodies, so that animals higher up the **food chain** contain larger and larger doses. A bird of prey such as an eagle, at

Measuring eggshells for the effects of the insecticide DDT.

An injured imperial eagle rescued by a ranger in an Indian national park.

the top of the chain, can receive a large dose in total during its lifetime.

Even if the pesticide does not kill the eagle, it interferes with its breeding. People did not know why this should be, until they discovered that birds affected by some pesticides lay eggs with very thin shells. The eggs break before they can hatch.

A particular danger to the bald eagle, where it survives in the United States, is oil. There was a dreadful example of this when the tanker *Exxon Valdez* was wrecked in Alaska in 1989.

Alaska is one of the last places where bald eagles are still common. They came to the beaches to scavenge the corpses of fish and sea otters which had died in the oil spill, and were themselves poisoned in large numbers.

Eagles and electricity

In the United States, eagles have a particular problem because they mistake electricity pylons for dead trees, and perch or build their nests on them. If a twig touches the live cable, or if the eagle's wing brushes against it, the eagle is electrocuted.

Protecting eagles

Eagles can be protected in several ways, depending on the problem they face. To stop farmers from killing them, it is necessary to explain to the farmers that eagles take very few domestic animals, if any. It is better to protect their animals while they are very small than to kill the eagles. During the rest of the year, the eagles actually help the farmer by taking pests such as rabbits and hares.

Explaining this will have a greater effect than making laws protecting eagles, and punishing people who harm them. Fines and imprisonment do not bring eagles back to life.

Poisoning by pesticides is still a danger. The worst of the chemicals are now banned in most developed countries, although they are still used in some poor countries. So long as these poisons are in the environment, eagles and all birds of prey will be in danger. Today, pesticides are tested before they are used, to try to make sure that they do not harm anything other than the pests that they are meant to kill.

Loss of habitat is more difficult to control, since people need places to live and to grow

Opposite *If eagles survive it is a sign that the land is in good condition.*

Below *Bald eagles are bred in captivity in the U.S.A.*

Saving eagles from electrocution

Eagles are now in much less danger from electricity in the United States, than they were in the past. The pylons have been redesigned so that the cables are further apart, and eagles can fly between them without touching. Also, engineers go out from time to time to trim the twigs of the eagles' nests, so that they do not touch the cables.

their food. However, farming and forestry can be done in a way that will leave more habitat for eagles and the animals they need for food.

Eagles should be protected, not least because they are a sign that the environment is in good condition. Even if there are people somewhere who do not appreciate the glory of eagles, their value as an environmental **indicator species** should be enough reason to make sure that they survive.

Glossary

Camouflaged Coloured so as to match the background, hard to see.
Canopy The top layer of leaves in a forest.
Carrion The flesh of dead animals.
Coat of arms A design, usually on a shield, to represent a family, city, or country.
Colonies Groups of animals living together.
Down The very fluffy feathers which are a chick's first covering.
Food chain A natural sequence which starts with plants which are eaten by small animals which are eaten by larger animals, which are preyed upon by even larger animals.
Gill An organ with very thin skin by which a fish collects oxygen to breathe when it is underwater.
Habitat The place which is most suitable for an animal's home.
Hyrax A small African mammal which lives in rocky country.
Immune Being able to resist poison or diseases.
Indicator species A plant or animal which shows by its good or bad condition whether the environment is doing well or badly.
Lectern Reading desk in a church.
Mammal An animal with warm blood, whose mother feeds it on milk when it is young.
Migrate Move regularly from one climate to another as the seasons change.

Northern hemisphere The half of the earth north of the equator.
Pesticides Chemicals used to poison insects or plants which damage crops.
Predator An animal that hunts and kills other animals.
Prey An animal which is hunted and eaten by another animal.
Rancher Someone who owns or works a large farm in North America.
Retina The layer of cells, like a screen, inside the back of the eye.
Scavenger An animal which eats the dead remains of other animals.
Soar Fly upwards in rising warm air, without moving the wings.
Spawning The laying and fertilising of eggs by fish or amphibians.
Superstition A belief that something will bring luck, either good or bad.
Talons The claws of a bird of prey.
Tendons Stringy pieces of gristle that connect muscles to bones.
Territory An area protected by an animal for its own use.
Thermal A column of rising warm air.
Trophy A dead animal displayed for other people to admire.
Wingspan The distance from wingtip to wingtip.

About the author

Malcolm Penny has a B.Sc. Hons degree in zoology from Bristol University and led the Bristol Seychelles Expedition in 1964. He was also a member of the Royal Society Expedition to Aldabra in 1966. Malcolm has worked for the Wildfowl Trust and was the First Scientific Administrator for I.C.B.P. on Cousin Island in the Seychelles. He now works as a producer of natural history programmes for Survival Anglia.

Index

The entries in **bold** are illustrations.

American Indians 24

beaks 4, **5**, 7
breeding 22, 23
buzzards 4
   African 6

camouflage 10
chicks 4, 18–19, **18**, 20
   feeding of **17**
courtship 16–17

eagles
   African short-toed 10, **10**, **11**, **23**
   as gods 24
   bald 9, **9**, 15, **15**, 20, **20**, 27, 28
   bateleur **21**
   booted **19**
   Congo serpent 12
   crowned 12, 14
   fish 8–9, **8**, 20
   golden 14, **14**, **19**, 24
   harpy 12, **13**, 14
   hunters of 25
   imperial **27**
   in Christianity 24
   martial 14
   Philippine 12, **12**
   snake 10–11, **10**
   spotted 23

steppe 23
tawny **7**, **22**, 23
Verreaux **7**
wedge-tailed 14
eaglets 19, **19**
eggs 18
eyesight 4, **5**, 6, 20

falcons 4
feathers 19
   down 19, **19**
   for archery 24
   in headdresses 24
   primaries 15
fighting 20
fishing 8–9
flyways 22
food 4, 11, **17**, 18, 20

Glacier National Park, USA

habitat 4, 5
   loss of 26–7, 28–9
Hawk Mountain, Pennsylvania 22
hawks 4
hunting 4, 6–7, 8, 9, 14, 15, 20, 26

legs 10

mantling, 7, **7**
migration 22–3, 25

nests 16–17, **16**, 19

owls 4

pesticides 26, **26**, 27, 28
predators 6, 16
prey 4–5, 6, **6**, 7, **7**, 8, 15, 23, 25, 28
   birds 4, 9
   carrion 9
   fish 4, 8, 20
   hyraxes 7, **7**
   grasshoppers 6
   mammals 4, 7
   monkeys 12
   rabbits and hares 7, 23, 25
   sheep 15
   snakes 4, 10–11
   sloths 12

Roman Empire, the 20

scavenging, 9, 20

talons 4, **4**, 8
   ornaments for good luck 24
territory 11, 16, 20

vultures 4

wings 6, 12, 15

Picture Acknowledgements

The publishers would like to thank the
Survival Anglia picture library
and the following photographers for the use
of photographs on the pages listed:

Jeff Foot 4,9,15,17,20,24,25,26,28,29,30; Jozef Mihok 5,16,18,19;
Dieter and Mary Plage 6,8,14; Alan Root 7,15; Bill Cowen 7; Cindy
Buxton 8; Cesallos/Kemp 11; Maurice Tibbles 12;
John Harris 13; Bamford & Borrill 14; Mike Tomkies 19; Bruce
Davidson 21; Richard and Julia Kemp 23; Jen and Des Bartlett 22;
Mike Price 27.